I CAN'T BE(LIEVE IT WORKED)

Combine Hypnosis with Breathwork to Access the Body and Mind, Rewire the Subconscious, and Grow Your Business

By Fabian Wesselink

Copyright © 2025 Fabian Wesselink

All rights reserved.

No part of this publication may be reproduced, distributed, or transmitted in any form or by any means, including photocopying, recording, or other electronic or mechanical methods, without the prior written permission of the author, except in the case of brief quotations used in critical reviews or educational settings.

For permission requests, please contact:

info@thebreatholution.com

This book is a work of nonfiction based on the author's personal experience and professional methodology. Some names and identifying details have been changed to protect privacy.

First edition Printed in Australia

Cover design by Robert Jarocki

Interior design by The Breatholution™ Team

ISBN: 9798294491918

CONTENTS

INTRODUCTION 1

CHAPTER 1: WHY YOUR BEST SESSIONS STILL
FEEL INCOMPLETE 7

CHAPTER 2: THE BREATH BEHIND THE
BREAKTHROUGH 15

CHAPTER 3: NERVOUS SYSTEMS SELL, NOT JUST
STRATEGIES 30

CHAPTER 4: THE FOUNDATION NOBODY TEACHES . . . 42

CHAPTER 5: THE BREATHOLUTION™ METHOD
TECHNIQUES THAT WILL CHANGE YOUR
PRACTICE FOREVER 57

CHAPTER 6: CONGRATS, YOU CREATED A JOB
(NOT A BUSINESS) 71

CHAPTER 7: FULL CIRCLE 92

INTRODUCTION

This book is short. Intentionally short.

Because transformation doesn't require more information—it requires the right information. And more importantly, it requires embodiment. I learned this in a Vipassana meditation retreat:

Knowledge is information you understand. Wisdom is truth you experience in your body.

In the next few hours, you'll discover what took me close to a decade and a fortune to learn the hard way.

Who This Book Is For

This book is specifically written for change-makers who are ready to revolutionize their approach and their business. You might be a well-established coach, wellness practitioner, hypnotherapist, or healer who's already making good money, but something feels fundamentally off. You're exhausted after sessions. The one-on-one work is draining you more than it should. You know there has to be a better way to create more impact without burning out your nervous system in the process.

Perhaps you're just starting out in the transformation space. You have the skills, the certifications, and the genuine passion to help people heal, but getting people to notice and pay for your work feels like pushing a boulder uphill. The schools taught you powerful techniques, but somehow for got to mention how to build a sustainable practice that feeds your soul and your bank account.

Maybe you're a breathwork facilitator who creates incredible experiences for people, but you've noticed that the insights and breakthroughs don't always integrate. People leave your sessions feeling transformed, but weeks later, they're back to their old patterns. You know something is missing from the equation, but you can't quite put your finger on what it is.

Or you could be a hypnotherapist who gets excellent results with some clients while others seem to hit an invisible wall. You've mastered the scripts and understand the subconscious mind, but there's a percentage of people who just don't seem to respond the way they should. You suspect their body is somehow blocking the transformation, but traditional hypnotherapy training never taught you how to work with that resistance.

If any of this resonates deeply, if you're nodding your head and thinking, "Finally, someone understands," then keep reading. This book will change how you practice forever.

Why This Book?

Let me share something that might shock you. Before discovering The Breatholution™ Method, I had done everything the transformation industry told me to do. I'm talking about three different NLP trainers. I learned techniques such as timeline therapy, parts integration, anchoring, reframing, and submodality work. You name the NLP technique, I'd mastered it.

I trained in hypnotherapy with multiple schools. Classical hypnosis, Ericksonian approaches, regression therapy, trauma therapy. I could put someone in a deep trance and install suggestions with textbook precision. I attended breakthrough seminars, where I danced in rooms filled with thousands of people. I walked on fire. I broke boards with my bare hands. I screamed until my voice was hoarse, releasing "limiting beliefs" that were supposedly holding me back.

I practiced rebirthing breathwork, holotropic breathwork, and Wim Hof breathing. I meditated daily. I journaled. I visualized. And you know what? After all of that training, all those certifications, all those breakthrough moments, all that money spent, I was still broke as a hypnotherapist. That's when I started thinking: Am I missing something? What am I missing?

This book exists for two reasons:

First, to encourage you to work with me and bring this incredible work to the world through my Breatholution™ Method certification program.

Second, to get you unstuck, get you moving, and demonstrate how The Breatholution™ Method actually works so you're more likely to do reason number one. But here's what's different: I'm not going to spend 200 pages convincing you. Instead, I'm going to show you exactly what works, give you tools you can use immediately, and let the results speak for themselves. At the very least, you'll walk away knowing that The Breatholution™ Method is solid because you'll get real results from what I share in these pages.

What You'll Discover

I've organized this book to take you on a specific journey, and here's why I've structured it this way. In Chapter 1, we'll explore why even your best sessions might feel incomplete and how working with the entire human system can change everything. In Chapter 2, we'll explore why mindset work alone isn't enough and examine the latest science on nervous system regulation. Chapter 3 gets honest about how your own trauma responses are either building or destroying your business. In Chapter 4, we'll delve into the foundational breathing principles that most practitioners never learn, along with my comprehensive 3-Phase Method. Chapter 5 gives you specific techniques that you can use immediately. Chapter 6 shows you how to scale beyond 1:1 sessions and build a sustainable transformation business. Finally, Chapter 7 brings everything full circle, exploring the ripple effects of this work.

In the chapters ahead, you'll learn:

- Why even your best sessions might be missing a crucial element.
- The science of nervous system regulation that changes everything.
- How to integrate breath and mind for transformations that actually stick.
- Specific techniques you can use in your very next session.
- Why 1:1 work (only) will keep you trapped (and what to do instead).
- How to build a practice that scales your impact without burning out.

A Personal Promise

I could tell you about the thousands of lives that have been impacted by The Breatholution™ Method. The hundreds of practitioners I'm training globally who are finally getting the breakthroughs they've been searching for. The stages I've spoken on from Europe to Vegas. The transformational retreats in Bali. The boardrooms in Sydney where executives are learning to breathe again. How I went from broke hypnotherapist to the owner of a multiple six-figure business. But testimonials and success stories are just words on a page.

Instead, I'm going to make you a simple promise: By the time you finish this book, you'll have at least one technique that will fundamentally change your next session. You'll understand why some transformations stick while others fade. And you'll see exactly why practitioners from all over the world join our weekly classes to learn this work. All I ask is that you test what you learn here. Try even one technique from Chapter 5. Feel the difference in your own body first! Because once you experience what breath and mind together can do, you'll never go back to working with incomplete systems again. Let's dive in.

CHAPTER 1

WHY YOUR BEST SESSIONS STILL FEEL INCOMPLETE

When was the last time a client left your session and immediately texted three friends about the transformation they just experienced? When did someone last look you in the eyes, voice cracking with emotion, and say, "That was one of the most memorable moments for me easily in the last at least ten years."

Or, when was the last time you had a really satisfying, life changing session with a practitioner yourself, one that left you fundamentally shifted rather than just temporarily inspired? If you're being honest, it's probably been a while. Or maybe never. And it's not your fault. You've been handed half a map and told it would take you all the way home. But there's a crucial piece that changes everything.

Let's Get Uncomfortably Honest

Every day, practitioners around the world guide clients through powerful sessions using proven techniques, such as cognitive behavioral therapy, neurolinguistic programming, timeline therapy, parts therapy, regression work, and the Emotional Freedom Technique. Let's get uncomfortably honest for a moment. It doesn't matter if you've been doing this work for 25 years or 25 days; you know exactly what I'm about to describe:

You've just delivered a textbook-perfect session. Used every technique. Hit every mark. Then your client opens their eyes and says those three words that make you die a little inside: "Nothing really happened." How many times have you felt that sinking feeling when they give you that polite smile that means nothing really shifted? Sure, some trainers tell you, "Not everyone is ready to change." or "Some people just resist doing the work." We could argue about that all day. But here's what I know: Since I started using The Breatholution™ Method, a systematic integration of breathwork and hypnosis that works with both the nervous system and subconscious mind simultaneously, I don't have those sessions anymore. Not one. People feel it. People shift. Every. Single. Time. What if the problem was never your client's resistance? What if you just didn't have all the tools?

Working With Half the Tools

Traditional approaches work brilliantly within their scope:

- Hypnotherapists create deep trance states and install new programming with remarkable precision.

- Breathwork facilitators activate the nervous system and release stored trauma through powerful somatic experiences.

- NLP practitioners reframe limiting beliefs and rewire thought patterns using elegant linguistic interventions.

- Coaches help clients clarify goals and overcome mental barriers through structured conversations and accountability.

All of these approaches work. The research proves it. The testimonials confirm it.

So, why do so many sessions feel... incomplete?

Traditional hypnotherapy accesses the subconscious mind beautifully, but often the body remains dysregulated, stuck in fight, flight, freeze, or fawn responses that create physical tension, shallow breathing, and nervous system activation. When the body sends danger signals at 20,000 impulses per second, new beliefs are installed on top of unresolved nervous system activation. It's like trying to plant seeds in concrete.

Pure breathwork activates and regulates the nervous system powerfully, creating profound somatic releases and altered states of consciousness. But without conscious integration of new beliefs and patterns, the transformation often doesn't stick. People feel amazing for a few days, then slide back into familiar thought patterns and behaviors.

Coaching and NLP excel at changing thought patterns and reframing limiting beliefs at the conscious level. But if the nervous system is stuck in fight-or-flight mode, sending constant signals that say "danger," the body overrides whatever the mind decides.

Each modality works with part of the human system. But lasting transformation requires working with the whole system. It's like trying to tune a guitar by only adjusting half the strings. No matter how perfectly you tune those three, the music will never sound quite right.

Here's What Actually Works

The Breatholution™ Method isn't hypnotherapy. It's not breathwork. It's not coaching or NLP. It's the integration of all of them, working simultaneously.

Think of it this way: Traditional approach: Mind or body.

The Breatholution™ Method approach: Mind and body, at the same time.

We use specific breathing patterns to activate and regulate the nervous system, creating what I call optimal states for subconscious receptivity. These optimal states include parasympathetic nervous system activation, which signals safety to the body; increased neuroplasticity, allowing old patterns to dissolve more easily; altered brainwave states similar to those achieved in deep meditation; and somatic activation, which moves stuck energy and emotion through the body naturally.

Then we install new programming while the body releases old patterns.

The breath activates. Heart rate shifts, muscles release, and the nervous system says, "It's safe now." The mind integrates. New beliefs land in a body that's actually ready to receive them. The transformation sticks because for the first time, every part of the system is saying "yes" at once.

When Body and Mind Finally Communicate

When you work with both the nervous system AND the subconscious simultaneously:

- Resistance drops because the body feels safe to let go.
- Trance states deepen naturally because activation opens receptivity.
- Emotional releases occur naturally because breathing creates space.
- New programming installs at a cellular level because it's embodied.
- Clients leave feeling transformed in every aspect, mind, body, and spirit.

This explains why people say things like:

"One session equals four hypnotherapy sessions." This is from someone who'd spent five years and thousands of dollars on traditional hypnotherapy.

"I've done hypnotherapy with some of the greatest hypnotherapists in the world. This was nothing like anything I've ever experienced before."

"Hypnosis alone can never do anything like this!"

Playing Piano With Both Hands

Most practitioners spend their entire career working with either the mind or the body. The Breatholution™ Method practitioners learn to access both simultaneously.

It's like the difference between playing piano with one hand versus two hands. You can tap out "Happy Birthday" with one finger, and people will recognize the tune. But when both hands work together, when the left hand grounds the rhythm while the right hand soars, that's when people stop what they're doing and really listen.

While other practitioners are trying to create change through talking and thinking, you'll create change through the body's own natural healing mechanisms. While they're spending months building rapport and trust, you'll create profound transformation in the first session. While they're competing on price and fighting for clients, you'll have people traveling hours to work with you because nobody else can deliver what you do.

20,000 Times Faster Than Your Thoughts

Here's what most practitioners never learn: Your nervous system processes information 20,000 times faster than your conscious mind. Let that sink in. While you're crafting the perfect hypnotic suggestion, your client's body has already decided whether it's safe to receive it.

Dr. Stephen Porges discovered that your body is constantly scanning for safety and danger through a process called "neuroception," an unconscious detection system that operates completely below the level of conscious awareness. This system continuously evaluates facial expressions, voice tone, body language, and environmental cues to determine whether it's safe to connect, learn, and change.

When someone's nervous system is dysregulated, when neuroception detects threat signals, it doesn't matter how brilliant your hypnotic suggestions are. The body's alarm system will override them every time, creating physical tension, mental resistance, and emotional shutdown that blocks the very transformation you're trying to facilitate. But when you regulate the nervous system first through breath, then engage the subconscious, magic happens. The body and mind work together instead of against each other.

Same Words, Different World

Traditional session: "Close your eyes and imagine feeling confident..."

The Breatholution™ Method session: "Breathe with me... feel that activation... Now, as your nervous system settles into safety, imagine confidence flowing through every cell of your body..."

Same suggestion. Completely different reception. Because the body is prepared to receive it.

But First, My Breaking Point

In the next chapter, I'll share the story of how this integration was discovered through my own breakdown and breakthrough, and how a broken promise to my five-year-old daughter led to a method that's now transforming practices around the world.

But first, you need to understand what The Breatholution™ Method actually is. Because once you see the logic of whole system integration, everything else makes perfect sense.

The question isn't whether this approach works. The question is: Are you ready to experience what happens when you stop working with part of the system and start working with all of it?

Because your next client is counting on it. They've tried everything else. Right now, they're building up the courage to book that session with you, whether they're sitting in their car outside your office or staring at your booking link online, hoping that maybe, just maybe, you'll be different.

Will you?

CHAPTER 2

THE BREATH BEHIND THE BREAKTHROUGH

The story that cracked it all open and created a method the industry wasn't ready for.

I walked out of that door and heard my five-year-old daughter's voice break behind me:

"Daddy, please, you promised! You promised!" That moment? I felt like I was dying inside.

Everything I thought I was, the father, the partner, the man my entire identity— collapsed right there on that doorstep. Just as my little girl's world crumbled, my world crumbled with it.

Just one week before, I had dropped to my knees, looked her straight in those innocent eyes, and said, "Irie, I will never leave you. I promise." This was after another massive fight with my ex-partner, whom I call the soulmate of the old version of me. Nineteen years together, but we couldn't make it work.

But there I was, walking out that door again.

Another fight. Another breakdown. The weight of everything crushing me. The fear gnawing at my gut: Will I ever see my daughter again? The devastating guilt toward my expartner, this woman I'd built a life with. And the shame...

God, the shame I felt toward my friends and my parents who taught me "You work problems out, you don't give up."

When the pain became so unbearable, I had two choices: transform or destroy everything I loved.

The Broken Promise That Became My Purpose

I'd already tried looking outside myself for answers. Using alcohol to numb the pain. Drugs to escape reality. Chasing validation to fill the void.

None of it worked. It just made everything worse. So, I chose transformation.

I threw myself into every healing modality I could find. Tony Robbins became my obsession. I dove into hypnotherapy training. NLP courses. Personal breakthrough sessions. And you know what? It worked. I became a certified hypnotherapist. I started getting clients. Some sessions were life-changing.

But something was eating at me.

Even with all my training and the breakthrough moments I was creating for others, I was still working construction during the day to pay the bills. I was still struggling financially. And here's the part that really messed with my head: I was still using alcohol to numb the pain. Still smoking the occasional joint to escape reality. Here I was, trying to help people transform their lives, while I was self-medicating just to get through my own days.

The incongruence was killing me.

How could I guide someone through releasing their addictions when I was still reaching for alcohol? How could I help them find inner peace when I needed weed to quiet my own racing mind? How could I facilitate their breakthroughs when I was still struggling myself?

The techniques I'd learned were powerful, but they weren't changing my life fast enough. And if I'm being brutally honest, some of my clients were still saying those three words that haunted me: "Nothing really happened."

Too often, clients would finish a session and say things like, "I don't think I was hypnotized" or "I'm not sure if it worked."

You know that feeling, right? When you've just guided someone through what you thought was powerful work, and they're looking at you like nothing happened? Even worse, some would ask for their money back.

They weren't fully dropping into the process. Something was preventing them from accessing that deeper state where real transformation happens. I knew there had to be a missing piece, but I had no clue what it was.

I had all the tools, all the certifications, all the knowledge, and did all the mindset work. But I was missing something fundamental. Something that would make transformation not just possible, but inevitable.

The Beach Transformation

Then one day, a mate invited me to "breathwork and ice baths" on a Sydney beach.

I laughed in his face.

"Mate," I said, "ice baths? Hell yes, sign me up. But breathwork? That's complete bullshit. I've been breathing my entire life, and I'm pretty damn good at it. What kind of nonsense is that?"

He insisted I come anyway. Thank God he did.

There I was, standing on this beach with about 50 people, listening to this woman share how breathing changed her life after struggling with anorexia. I stood there thinking, "What a load of crap. Breathing changed your life? Really?"

Then we started….

Ten minutes of conscious breathing. That's it.

And what happened next completely blew my mind.

For the first time in my entire life, my monkey mind, that constant, never-ending chatter, that endless conversation with myself, went completely quiet. Dead silent.

I felt this peace I'd never experienced before. Energy was flowing through my body like electricity. I was seeing colors. I felt connected to something way bigger than myself.

I was completely hooked.

I rushed home and jumped straight online: "What the hell is this breathwork thing? I need to know everything."

I found a practitioner and booked a session immediately. And what happened is quite hard to describe if you've never experienced activation breathwork. I thought I was healed from all my therapy work, the NLP breakthroughs, all those hypnotherapy sessions, the shadow work. I genuinely believed I was ready to help others after all that work.

Boy, was I wrong.

The Vision

In that one breathwork session, something was unleashed that I wasn't prepared for. I cried harder than I'd cried in years, tears that felt like they were coming from my soul, from places I didn't even know existed. Grief that I had no idea I was carrying poured out of me like a dam had burst. Rage surfaced from places I'd forgotten existed. My entire body shook uncontrollably, vibrating like electricity was coursing through every single cell. Decades of stored trauma was finally finding its way out.

And right in the middle of that session, I saw myself. Clear as day. Standing on stages around the world, facilitating this work with hundreds of people.

That vision? It changed everything.

It wasn't just a nice thought or wishful thinking. It was so vivid, so real, that I could feel the energy of those crowds, hear the sounds of people breathing together, and sense the collective transformation happening in those rooms. I knew with absolute certainty that this was my path.

But I had no idea I was about to accidentally create something the industry had never seen before.

The Accidental Innovation

I immediately found a teacher and got certified in breathwork. But something magical was happening that I didn't even realize. I wasn't just doing "breathwork" like everyone else. I was naturally weaving in everything I'd learned, the hypnotherapy language patterns, the NLP techniques, the timeline work, all that subconscious reprogramming stuff.

I didn't even know I was doing it. It just felt... right. Natural.

While people were in these altered states from the breathing, with their defenses completely down and their nervous systems wide open, I'd find myself guiding them through visualizations. Installing new beliefs. Using metaphors and suggestions that would normally take weeks to land in traditional hypnosis.

And people noticed. Boy, did they notice.

Some were traveling two hours to come to my sessions. Two bloody hours! To Sydney, where you could find breathwork and ice baths on multiple beaches every weekend. When I asked them why they'd make that crazy journey, what they told me stopped me dead in my tracks:

"Your breathwork is different, Fabian."

"Your sessions take me way deeper than anyone else."

"There's something about the way you guide that just... transforms me."

But the comment that really blew my mind came from a client who said: "I've done hypnotherapy sessions with some of the greatest hypnotherapists in the world. This was unlike anything I had ever experienced before. No professional hypnotherapist has ever brought me into a state this deep, this profound, this transformative."

Eventually, people started asking me to teach them. Not regular breathwork, they wanted to learn how I did it. My way. My method.

That's when it hit me like a freight train: I'd accidentally created something different, something completely new.

Your Thoughts Can't Change What Your Body Still Believes

What I discovered through this journey was the truth I shared in Chapter 1: Your nervous system processes information 20,000 times faster than your conscious mind. So while you're up in your head trying to think positive thoughts or visualize success, your body is already flooded with signals about whether it's safe to receive those new ideas.

I wasn't just teaching this concept. I was living it. My body was still holding all the trauma from walking out on Irie. All the shame, guilt, and fear were trapped in my nervous system, sabotaging every attempt I made to build the life I wanted.

Traditional hypnosis was trying to access my subconscious while my nervous system was screaming, "DANGER!" But breathwork? Breathwork regulated my nervous system first, creating a sense of safety, and then allowed the new programming to take hold.

That's when I realized: If I couldn't regulate my own nervous system first, how could I expect to help others do the same?

The Integration Breakthrough

I'd combined conscious breathing with hypnosis and all the change work techniques I'd learned. I was accessing the nervous system through breath, then reprogramming the subconscious while people were in that activated state.

Traditional hypnosis works by accessing altered states of consciousness through various induction methods. The Breatholution™ Method creates these states through activation. Instead of trying to quiet the mind, we activate the body so powerfully that the mind has no choice but to step aside.

I was creating breakthroughs in one session that used to take months.

The Breatholution™ Method was born.

And I finally understood why my traditional sessions sometimes fell flat. I was working with half the system, trying to reprogram the mind while the body was still dysregulated. It was like trying to unlock a door with half a key.

Van der Kolk vs. Barrett: They're Both Right

What I'd stumbled onto through my own experience aligned perfectly with the two major schools of thought in trauma and transformation work.

Dr. Bessel van der Kolk's research shows that trauma is stored in the body itself. His work demonstrates that traumatic experiences live in muscle tension, breathing patterns, posture, and nervous system responses. According to van der Kolk, you must work directly with the body through movement, breathwork, and somatic practices to discharge trapped survival energy.

Dr. Lisa Feldman Barrett's neuroscience research reveals that emotions are predictions our brain makes based on past experiences. Her work shows that trauma exists in the brain's predictive patterns, and we can rewire these patterns through cognitive restructuring and conscious awareness.

Both approaches have compelling evidence. Both have helped millions of people. And both are missing something crucial when used alone.

Van der Kolk's approach focuses on somatic healing but sometimes misses the cognitive reprogramming that helps people integrate new meaning-making frameworks. Barrett's approach emphasizes changing brain patterns, but it doesn't always address the body's stored responses that continue to send alarm signals.

The Breatholution™ Method honors both simultaneously. The breath regulates the nervous system and releases stored trauma (van der Kolk). The hypnotic elements reprogram predictive patterns and install new beliefs (Barrett). Together, they create transformation that sticks at every level.

The Highway to Healing

Your vagus nerve, the longest nerve in your body, is the highway between your body and brain. And here's the part that revolutionized my practice: 80 percent of the vagus nerve fibers carry information FROM the body TO the brain. Only 20 percent of the information travels from the brain to the body.

Your body is sending four times more information to your brain than your brain sends to your body.

Traditional therapy uses the 20 percent pathway, trying to think your way into feeling better. The Breatholution™ Method utilizes the 80 percent superhighway, allowing you to breathe your way into new states that the mind can then embrace.

This realization changed everything for me. Instead of trying to think my way out of the pain of breaking my promise to Irie, I started breathing my way through it.

The "Aha" Moment That Changes Everything for Practitioners

Breathwork alone is already phenomenal. It creates profound states, emotional releases, and nervous system shifts that can be life-changing.

But when you start adding hypnosis during the breathwork, when you begin combining NLP techniques while people are in these activated states, and when you weave in sub conscious reprogramming while their defenses are completely down, that's when the magic happens. That's when you get those amazing outcomes that have people saying, "What just happened? That changed everything."

The breakthrough wasn't just the discovery of breathwork. Thousands of people know breathwork. The breakthrough was realizing that most practitioners are using incomplete systems.

They're either working with the mind (hypnosis, NLP, coaching) OR the body (breathwork, somatic work), but rarely both simultaneously.

It's like trying to unlock a door with half a key.

Great Release, But Then What?

Pure breathwork is incredibly powerful. It activates the nervous system, creates emotional releases, and shifts brainwave states. People cry, shake, laugh, and experience profound insights. They leave feeling transformed.

But without conscious integration of new beliefs and patterns, the transformation often doesn't stick. The nervous system returns to baseline, and old thought patterns reassert themselves; within weeks, people find themselves back where they started.

Breathwork opens the door to transformation. But someone needs to walk through it with conscious intention and new programming.

Painting Over Rust

Traditional hypnosis excels at accessing the subconscious and installing new programming. Skilled hypnotherapists create deep trance states and embed suggestions with precision. New beliefs get installed directly into the subconscious database.

But without somatic activation and nervous system regulation, the new programming sits on top of unresolved activation. The suggestions are there, but the body's alarm system continues broadcasting danger signals that override the new programming.

It's like painting over rust. It looks good temporarily, but the underlying corrosion continues eating away at the foundation.

What I discovered through my own breakdown became The Breatholution™ Method. Not just a technique, but a complete framework for transformation that honors both the body's wisdom and the mind's power.

This method didn't just change my practice. It saved my life. It gave me the tools to finally heal the trauma of that broken promise. It allowed me to regulate my nervous system so I could show up as the father Irie deserved. It transformed my relationship with my expartner from one of guilt and shame to one of respect and coparenting collaboration.

Most importantly, it gave me a way to help others that actually worked. Consistently. Powerfully. Completely.

No more clients saying, "Nothing happened." No more sessions that felt incomplete. No more wondering if the transformation would stick.

Feel First, Think Later

The industry is shifting toward nervous system work because we're finally understanding that transformation isn't just a mental process. It's a whole-system process that must include the body's wisdom.

Your thoughts don't create your reality. Your nervous system state creates your reality, and then your thoughts follow.

When someone is in a state of nervous system safety, they naturally think positive, abundant thoughts (LOVE). When they're in fight or flight, they think anxious, overwhelming thoughts. When they're in freeze, they think hopelessly, "what's the point" thoughts (FEAR).

The state comes first. The thoughts follow. But the thoughts also reinforce the state, creating either upward spirals of expansion or downward spirals of contraction.

All In, Not Half and Half

Most practitioners believe that transformation is 80 percent mental and 20 percent physical, or vice versa.

Complete transformation requires 100 percent nervous system activation AND 100 percent cognitive reprogramming, integrated simultaneously.

Get someone into a regulated, activated state through breath, and their mind becomes incredibly receptive to new programming. Install new programming while their body is releasing old patterns, and both aspects reinforce each other, creating change that sticks at every level.

This explains why traditional approaches often plateau. Why breathwork experiences sometimes don't stick. Why hypnosis sessions can feel incomplete.

They're working with part of the system instead of the whole system.

The Promise I Try To Keep Every Day

Today, I keep the promise I made to Irie in a different way. Not by never leaving physically, but by never leaving the work of becoming the man, the father, the practitioner who shows up fully present and regulated.

Every practitioner I train, every breakthrough session I facilitate, every nervous system that learns to regulate through this work is my way of honoring that broken promise and turning it into purpose.

That beach in Sydney, that ten-minute miracle, that vision of stages around the world, it all led me here. To this work. To this method. To the understanding that healing happens when we stop choosing between the mind and body and start working with both.

In the next chapter, I'll reveal exactly how nervous system states are either building or destroying your business, and why the practitioners who understand this become the ones clients can't stop talking about.

Because your trauma response isn't just affecting your personal life. It's running your entire business.

CHAPTER 3

NERVOUS SYSTEMS SELL, NOT JUST STRATEGIES

Your trauma response is preventing your launch.

Something I see constantly in my programs: Practitioners show up who've already done "all the work." They've hired business coaches. They've taken marketing courses. They know their niche, their ideal client, and their pricing strategy. Some even have beautiful websites and perfect sales funnels.

But there's a problem.

They stopped working on themselves.

They learned their modalities, including hypnotherapy, NLP, coaching, breathwork, and then immediately shifted their focus to helping others. Meanwhile, their own nervous system regulation, their own trauma responses, and their own limiting beliefs? Those got put on the back burner.

Sound familiar?

High in the Room, Crashed at Home

Have you ever been to a Tony Robbins event? Or any high energy transformation workshop?

You know that feeling, right? You're surrounded by thousands of people, the energy is electric, the music is pumping, and you feel unstoppable. You're on cloud nine. You've broken through every limitation. You're ready to conquer the world.

Then you go home.

Back to your regular environment. Back to your relationships, your daily routines, your old triggers. And within days, maybe hours, you start sliding back into old patterns.

Now imagine this scenario: What if you went home to an abusive relationship? How long do you think that Tony Robbins high would last?

Probably about as long as it takes to walk through your front door.

This is exactly what happens to practitioners who stop doing their own work. They learned powerful transformation tools, but they never addressed their own internal environment, their nervous system patterns, their unconscious beliefs, and their trauma responses.

So, they try to build a business from the same dysregulated state in which they've always operated. They attempt to create abundance while their nervous system is stuck in scarcity mode. They try to be visible and powerful while their body is screaming, "Hide, it's not safe."

The external strategies don't work because the internal foundation isn't solid. You can't out-strategy your nervous system. When your internal alarm system is activated, it will sabotage the best business plan in the world.

Healed Enough to Help Others, Too Triggered to Help Yourself

Here's what's fascinating and heartbreaking at the same time: these practitioners can guide others through profound transformations. They know exactly what to say, which techniques to use, and how to hold space for difficult emotions. They can spot their clients' patterns from a mile away and facilitate breakthrough sessions that change lives.

However, when it comes to their own business, visibility, and success, they're a complete mess.

They'll spend an hour helping a client release money blocks, then go home and panic about their own pricing. They'll confidently guide someone through trauma healing, then freeze when it's time to post on social media about their services. They'll facilitate powerful breakthrough sessions for others, then sabotage their own launch right before it goes live.

It's like being a brilliant surgeon who can operate on everyone except themselves. They have the skills and understand the process, but when they're the patient, their own nervous system takes over, and chaos ensues.

Healing Isn't a Destination

Most practitioners think healing is a destination rather than a practice. They believe that once they've addressed their major trauma, completed their training, or had their big breakthrough, they're done. They can check "personal healing" off their list and focus on building their business.

But nervous system regulation isn't a one-time achievement. It's an ongoing practice, especially when you're stepping into bigger levels of visibility, success, and impact. Each new level of growth will trigger whatever unhealed patterns are still lurking in your system.

Think about it. If you've been playing small your whole life because visibility felt dangerous, what do you think happens when you start marketing yourself? If you've always struggled with money because abundance feels unsafe in your family, what gets activated when you start charging premium prices? If you learned early that your needs didn't matter, how does that show up when you're trying to set boundaries with demanding clients?

Every expansion triggers the next layer of healing. The practitioners who understand this stay ahead of the curve. The ones who don't get blindsided by their own unconscious patterns.

What Happens When Healers Stop Healing

When you stop working on yourself, several things happen:

- **Your nervous system defaults to old patterns:** Without regular regulation practices, you'll unconsciously slip back into fight, flight, freeze, or fawn responses when triggered.

- **Your energy becomes incongruent:** You're teaching about abundance while operating from a scarcity mindset. You're facilitating confidence while feeling insecure. People sense this misalignment.

- **Your capacity shrinks:** Instead of expanding your ability to hold bigger challenges, you start avoiding anything that feels too big or scary.

- **Your business reflects your internal state:** Chaotic inner world = chaotic business. Regulated inner world = sustainable, scalable business

Booked Solid With Clients, Empty on Self-Care

Most practitioners fall into what I call the "Self-Healing Gap." They're so focused on serving others that they stop prioritizing their own transformation. They'll book their calendar full of client sessions but skip their own therapy appointments. They'll invest thousands in business training but won't spend money on their own healing work.

This isn't noble. It's self-sabotage.

You can't give what you don't have. You can't lead others where you haven't been. And you can't build a business that exceeds your own level of nervous system regulation.

Think about it: If your nervous system can only handle

$5,000 months, what happens when you have a $15,000 launch? If your system can only manage ten clients, what occurs when 25 people want to work with you? If you can only tolerate a certain level of visibility, what gets triggered when your work starts gaining real attention?

Your nervous system will find ways to bring you back to your set point. Illness at crucial moments. Technical failures during important launches. Self-sabotage behaviors right before big opportunities. Relationship drama that demands your attention when you should be focusing on business growth.

She Let Go Because You Did First

One of my certified practitioners shared this testimonial that perfectly illustrates what happens when we do the ongoing work:

"Session went super well! She said: This is the first time in my life that I felt that it was all about me. There was always someone else I took into account, whom I pleased. And she also said she thought I did it like I do it for a long time. Big tears, shaking body, she let go of a lot! It felt quiet in her after the session and she believed for the first time the things that came out of her mouth, her critical voice was quiet"

This practitioner could facilitate this level of transformation because she'd done her own work on people-pleasing, making herself matter, and quieting her own critical voice.

The depth you can take your clients is directly proportional to the depth you've gone yourself.

Fight, Flight, Freeze, or Fawn: Pick Your Business Poison

Fight Response in Business:

- Aggressive marketing that turns people off.
- Pushy sales conversations that create resistance.
- Competing instead of collaborating with other practitioners.
- Burning out from trying to force results through sheer effort.

Flight Response in Business:

- Jumping from strategy to strategy without finishing anything.
- Constantly seeking the "next big thing" instead of mastering what you have.
- Avoiding difficult conversations with clients or team members.
- Starting projects but never completing them.

Freeze Response in Business:

- Knowing exactly what to do but being unable to take action.
- Perfectionism that prevents you from ever launching.
- Analysis paralysis around every business decision.
- Staying invisible because visibility feels too scary.

Fawn Response in Business:

- Giving everything away for free to avoid confrontation.
- Over-delivering to the point of exhaustion and resentment.
- Inability to set boundaries with demanding clients.
- Apologizing for your prices instead of owning your value.

Each of these responses made sense at some point in your life. They kept you safe when you actually were in danger. But when they're running your business, they create the very problems they're trying to protect you from.

Why Regulated Practitioners Get All the Referrals

Practitioners who maintain their own healing practice have an unfair advantage:

- **In marketing:** Their content feels authentic because they're living what they teach.

- **In sales:** Their conversations flow naturally because they're not desperate for outcomes.

- **In sessions:** They can hold deeper space because they're not triggered by client activation.

- **In pricing:** They charge what they're worth because they've done their own money work.

- **In scaling:** They can handle increased success without self-sabotaging.

The result is that their business becomes magnetic. People refer others to them not just because they get good results, but because the entire experience of working with them feels different. Clients leave feeling seen, held, and transformed, and they naturally want to share that experience with others.

Inner Peace, Outer Success

When you create an internal environment of regulation, safety, and abundance, it gets reflected in your external world. Your business becomes a natural extension of your inner state rather than a battle against it.

But this requires ongoing maintenance, like regular nervous system regulation through breathwork, movement, or other somatic practices, continuous trauma healing that addresses whatever gets triggered as you grow, and consistent work on your own limiting beliefs and patterns that emerge at each new level.

Most practitioners resist this because they think it takes time away from building their business. But the opposite is true. Your nervous system regulation IS your business development. Your personal healing work IS your marketing strategy. Your inner work IS your competitive advantage.

Think about it: Would you rather spend a few hours a week maintaining your internal foundation, or spend months recovering from the burnout and self-sabotage that happens when that foundation crumbles?

This is why The Breatholution™ Method isn't just about learning techniques to use with clients; it's about cultivating a deeper understanding of the breath. It's about creating a practice that keeps you regulated, embodied, and operating from your highest self.

When you breathe with intention, move trapped energy from your own system, and reprogram your own subconscious patterns, your business transforms automatically. Not because you're forcing it to change, but because you're changing the internal environment from which it emerges.

Your regulated nervous system becomes your greatest business asset. Your own healing journey becomes your most powerful marketing message. Your personal transformation becomes the foundation for everything you build.

When Did You Last Cry in a Session? (Your Own)

Let me ask you something that might make you uncomfortable: When was the last time you did deep healing work on yourself? Not for your clients, but for you? When did you last have a session where you cried, released, and broke through to a new level of self-acceptance and nervous system capacity?

If it's been more than a few months, your business is probably reflecting that neglect. The areas where you've stopped growing are the areas where your business will stop growing. The patterns you haven't healed are the patterns that will show up in your client relationships, pricing, marketing, and ability to hold space for success.

You might be getting away with it for now, especially if you're just starting out or playing small. But the bigger you want to build, the more your unhealed patterns will get triggered, and the more they'll sabotage your progress.

The Healers Who Never Stop Healing

In the next chapter, I'll show you the exact 3-Phase Method that integrates ongoing self-healing with business building, so you never have to choose between taking care of yourself and taking care of your business.

Because the most successful practitioners aren't the ones who "finished" their healing. They're the ones who made healing a lifelong practice.

And that practice becomes the foundation for everything else they build.

CHAPTER 4

THE FOUNDATION NOBODY TEACHES

I don't know about you, but I'd rather start with the root instead of putting a band-aid on someone.

Most people in the world are dysfunctional breathers. And this dysfunction creates a cascade of symptoms that practitioners are trying to fix with surface-level interventions. We're spending months working on anxiety without looking at the breathing patterns that are creating the physiology of panic. We're addressing depression without examining the shallow, restricted breathing that's starving the brain of optimal oxygen. We're treating insomnia without considering the mouth breathing that's keeping the nervous system in fight or flight all night long.

It's like trying to fix a flooded basement without turning off the water main. You can mop all day, but until you address the source, you're just managing symptoms.

The foundation of lasting transformation isn't positive thinking or even emotional release. It's functional breathing. And most practitioners have never been taught how to assess it, let alone restore it. This chapter will change that and revolutionize how you approach every client, including yourself.

Before we dive into the solution, you need to understand the scope of the problem. Most of your clients are walking around with multiple levels of breathing dysfunction that are sabotaging every intervention you attempt.

Physiological Dysfunction:

- No proper use of the diaphragm.
- Chest breathing, erratic breathing patterns.
- Moving the body while breathing.
- Shallow, restricted breathing patterns.

Cadence Dysfunction:

- Taking way too many breaths per minute. (12-20+ instead of 6-8)
- Chronic hyperventilation that depletes CO_2 levels.
- Fast, erratic breathing patterns that signal danger to the nervous system.

Biochemical Dysfunction:

- Chronic over-breathing that creates oxidative stress.
- Poor carbon dioxide tolerance.

- Improper oxygen delivery to cells. (The Bohr Effect)

All of this dysfunction is happening below the level of conscious awareness, approximately 20,000 to 24,000 times per day. And most practitioners never address it, never even assess it, because they've never been taught that breathing is the foundation of everything else they're trying to accomplish.

We Work on Everything Except the One Thing That Happens 24,000 Times Per Day

Knowing this, isn't it ridiculous that hypnotherapists and coaches want to help people quit smoking without looking at the 20,000 to 24,000 breaths they take per day?

Breathing is the first thing we do when we arrive on this planet, and it's the last thing we're going to do before we leave. It's happening 24/7, influencing every system in your body: your nervous system, cardiovascular system, immune system, digestive system, and hormonal system.

Breath is the only autonomic system that can be controlled both consciously and unconsciously. Your heart rate, digestion, and hormone production happen automatically. But breathing? You can take conscious control of it at any time, which makes it your direct pathway to influence your nervous system, emotional state, mental clarity, and physical health.

This is why traditional approaches often feel incomplete. They try to change the mind without addressing the foundation that creates the mental and emotional states in the first place.

They Are Doing Breathwork (With Cancer Sticks)

Ask any smoker why they smoke, and most will tell you: "It helps me relax." What are they actually doing? Taking a deep breath in, holding it, then slowly exhaling. They're unconsciously using breath to regulate their nervous system. They just happen to be doing it with a cancer stick in their hand.

This perspective completely changes how you approach smoking cessation. Smoking is breathwork. Just dysfunctional breathwork.

If you're treating smoking addiction without understanding this breathing mechanism, you're missing the entire foundation of the habit. You're trying to take away their primary nervous system regulation tool without giving them a healthier replacement.

The solution isn't to eliminate their breathing practice. It's to optimize it. Teach them functional breathing patterns that create the same nervous system regulation they're getting from cigarettes, but without the toxicity. Give them a healthier way to achieve the same physiological state they're seeking.

You Can't Think Your Way Out of a Panic Attack

When I was learning hypnotherapy for anxiety treatment, no one talked about breathing. No one mentioned breath work. Looking back, this seems almost insane given what we now know about the physiology of anxiety.

Think about this: In most cases, anxiety is actually a result of a breathing disorder. When someone has a panic attack, what's the first thing that happens? Their breathing becomes rapid, shallow, and chaotic. Then comes the racing heart, the sweating, the sense of doom, the feeling that they're going to die or lose control.

Yet most anxiety treatments focus on thoughts, beliefs, and coping strategies while completely ignoring the breathing patterns that are driving the physiology of panic. We try to calm the mind while the body is flooded with stress hormones triggered by dysfunctional breathing.

You can't think your way out of a panic attack. But you can breathe your way out of one.

This is exactly why so many transformation methods fall short. They address symptoms while ignoring the foundation that creates them. It's like trying to stop a fire alarm from beeping without addressing the smoke that's triggering it.

Bessel van der Kolk's Latest Approach

It is completely pointless to start working with anyone if we do not look at their breathing first.

Dr. Bessel van der Kolk, author of *The Body Keeps the Score,* has evolved his approach based on years of additional research and clinical experience. While his earlier work focused primarily on trauma's impact on the body through various somatic interventions, he now states: "For me, there's no point of doing any form of change work without looking at their breath. The first thing I do is look at their breathing."

This is revolutionary coming from someone who's spent decades in trauma therapy and has explored every modality imaginable. He's recognizing what we've always known in The Breatholution™ Method: Breath is the foundation of everything.

When the world's leading trauma expert says you must assess breathing before attempting any other intervention, it's time to listen. Your breathing patterns are either supporting your healing or sabotaging it. There's no neutral ground.

Test Yourself

Before you can help others optimize their breathing, you need to understand your own breathing patterns. This simple assessment will reveal more about your nervous system health than any questionnaire or psychological evaluation.

This is best done as a morning routine, before consuming caffeine or engaging in any stimulating activities. After waking up, take a few normal breaths to settle, then:

The Breath Foundation Score:

Take a normal breath in through your nose. Exhale normally out through your nose.

When you're about to take a breath in again, pinch your nose at the end of the exhalation.

Hold until you feel the definite urge to breathe. This isn't about holding as long as possible or creating discomfort. You're looking for the first clear signal from your body that it wants air.

Release your nose and return to normal breathing. No puffing out or gasping for air, just return to your natural rhythm.

Time this hold using a stopwatch on your phone or by counting seconds steadily.

Your score:

Under 15 seconds equals severely dysfunctional breathing patterns that are creating chronic stress in your system.

Fifteen to 25 seconds equals dysfunctional breathing that's limiting your capacity and keeping your nervous system slightly activated.

Twenty-five to 35 seconds equals functional baseline breathing that supports basic health and nervous system regulation.

Thirty-five-plus seconds equals optimal breathing function that enhances performance, clarity, and resilience.

Most practitioners I work with initially score between 10 to 20 seconds, which explains why they feel tired despite getting enough sleep, why they get triggered easily, and why their energy crashes throughout the day. The good news is that this can be trained and improved dramatically with consistent practice.

Dry Mouth Equals Danger Signal

Healthy breathing has one non-negotiable requirement it happens through your nose.

There are over 30 functions of nasal breathing, ranging from filtering and humidifying air to producing nitric oxide, which enhances oxygen delivery. There are zero benefits of chronic mouth breathing.

Simple test: Do you wake up in the morning with a dry mouth?

If so, that's an indication of a fight-or-flight response that has been active all night long. It means you were mouth breathing during sleep, which signals danger to your nervous system. For the seven to eight hours you thought you were resting and recovering, your body was actually lying there in a state of perceived threat.

Your sympathetic nervous system was activated throughout the night. No wonder you wake up tired despite "getting enough sleep." Your sleep wasn't actually restorative because your breathing patterns were keeping your system in survival mode.

This also explains why some people wake up with anxiety, why they feel groggy and foggy-headed in the morning, and why they need caffeine just to feel normal. Their breathing has been sabotaging their recovery all night long.

The Miracle Molecule in Your Nose

Here's something else most don't teach: Nitric oxide, the miracle molecule that won a Nobel Prize, could change everything about how you breathe and how you guide others.

In 1998, three scientists won the Nobel Prize for discovering nitric oxide's role as a signaling molecule in the cardiovascular system. Ongoing research continues to reveal that this molecule, produced primarily in the nasal passages, is crucial for optimal oxygen delivery to the brain and body.

When you breathe through your nose, you're not just filtering air. You're accessing this Nobel Prize winning molecule that dilates blood vessels for better oxygen flow, has antibacterial and antiviral properties that support immune function, improves cognitive function and mental clarity, enhances athletic performance and recovery, and supports overall cardiovascular health.

This is yet another reason why mouth breathing is robbing you and your clients of optimal health and performance. Every mouth breath bypasses this natural pharmacy in your nose, depriving your system of a molecule that evolution specifically designed to optimize your physiology.

Nitric oxide benefits include:

- Dilating blood vessels for better oxygen flow.
- Antibacterial and antiviral properties.
- Improved cognitive function.
- Enhanced athletic performance.
- Enhanced immune function.

Look, getting your breathing right is just the starting point. Yes, it's the foundation everything else builds on, but if you think I'm going to stop there, you don't know me very well.

In our practitioner program, we go way beyond just teaching people how to breathe properly. We show coaches, hypnotherapists, and wellness practitioners how to use breath as the ultimate vehicle for creating transformation, facilitating breakthroughs, and building the kind of business that actually sustains you.

That's why everything I teach follows a simple but powerful structure:

The 3 Phase Method: BREATHE. BREAKTHROUGH. BUILD.™

Phase 1: BREATHE (Regulate the Foundation)

This phase focuses on establishing nervous system safety and promoting optimal breathing function. You cannot build anything sustainable on a dysregulated foundation, regardless of how advanced your techniques or how strong your business strategy may be.

For you as a practitioner, this means learning functional breathing patterns that you can use throughout your day and developing daily regulation practices that keep your system balanced regardless of external pressures. Most importantly, it means regulating yourself before every client session so you can show up in your most grounded, present state, rather than your triggered or stressed state.

For your clients, this phase involves assessing their breathing function using simple tests, such as the one you just learned. It also involves creating safety in your sessions through your own regulated presence and clear boundaries, and building their foundation for transformation by teaching them basic breathing skills that they can use outside of sessions.

Key insight: Most practitioners skip this phase and wonder why their advanced techniques don't stick. You must regulate before you activate. You cannot create lasting change from a dysregulated state, whether that's your state or your client's.

Phase 2: BREAKTHROUGH *(Activate and Transform)*

This is where the magic happens. In this phase, you'll use the breath to access altered states and create rapid transformation through integrated change work that addresses both the nervous system and the subconscious mind.

For you as a practitioner, this means experiencing your own breakthrough sessions regularly so you continue expanding your capacity and clearing your blocks. It means clearing your money stories, visibility fears, and success blocks as they arise. Most importantly, it means embodying the transformation you teach so your work comes from authentic experience rather than theoretical knowledge.

For your clients, this phase involves using breath to bypass conscious resistance and access deeper states of receptivity, working with both somatic activation and cognitive reprogramming in the same session, releasing stored trauma and emotional blocks that have been limiting their growth, and creating profound shifts in single sessions that would normally take months of traditional therapy.

Key insight: *Breakthrough without integration is just a temporary high.* The breath activates and creates the optimal state, but conscious work integrates the change and makes it permanent.

Phase 3: BUILD (Integrate and Scale)

This phase is about turning transformation into sustainable success, both personally and professionally. It's about building systems and practices that maintain your growth and allow you to scale your impact without burning out your nervous system.

For you as a practitioner, this means building a business from a regulated nervous system, rather than from a state of survival. It means scaling your impact through group work and programs, rather than just trading time for money. Most importantly, it means maintaining your own healing practice while serving others, so that your business growth doesn't trigger old patterns or create new trauma.

For your clients, this phase involves integrating their breakthroughs into daily life through practical applications and new habits, building new patterns from their new identity rather than trying to maintain change through willpower, and developing their own regulation skills so they can handle life's challenges without losing their center.

Key insight: Most people experience breakthroughs but fail to establish systems to sustain them. This phase ensures lasting change that compounds over time rather than fading back to old patterns.

Skip a Phase, Hit a Wall

Each phase builds on the previous one, and trying to skip ahead will create predictable problems:

Without *BREATHE*, you're trying to create change from a dysregulated state. This is exhausting and unsustainable. You might get temporary results, but they won't last because the foundation isn't solid.

Without *BREAKTHROUGH*, you have regulation but no transformation. You're comfortable but not growing. You might feel better, but you're not actually changing the patterns that created your problems in the first place.

Without *BUILD*, you have transformation but no integration. This creates temporary change that fades over time. You might have powerful experiences, but they don't translate into lasting improvements in your life or business.

Together, you have a sustainable transformation that compounds over time. Your healing supports your growth, your growth deepens your healing, and both contribute to building something meaningful in the world.

Most healing modalities focus on one phase. Traditional therapy often stays in *BREATHE*, focusing on regulation and safety without creating breakthrough experiences. Intensive workshops focus on *BREAKTHROUGH*, creating powerful transformation experiences without teaching integration skills. Business coaching emphasizes *BUILD*, teaching systems and strategies without addressing the nervous system patterns that sabotage implementation.

The Breatholution™ Method integrates all three because you need all three for lasting change that improves your life, rather than providing temporary relief.

Which Phase Are You Neglecting?

Look at your own life and practice right now and honestly assess where you stand:

BREATHE: Is your nervous system regulated on a daily basis? Do you have consistent practices that keep you grounded and centered? Can you stay present under pressure, or do you get triggered and reactive?

BREAKTHROUGH: When was the last time you had a profound personal transformation? Are you still growing and expanding, or are you just maintaining your current level? Do you regularly work on your own blocks and patterns?

BUILD: Are you successfully translating your healing into sustainable business growth? Do you have systems in place to support your expansion? Can you scale your impact without burning out your nervous system?

Most practitioners are strong in one area but weak in the others. The 3-Phase Method ensures you develop all three simultaneously, creating a foundation for sustained success and impact.

15 Minutes That Change Everything Else

Each phase requires consistent practice, but it doesn't have to consume your life:

BREATHE requires 10 to 15 minutes of regulated breathing daily. This isn't another thing to add to your already busy schedule. This IS your stress management, energy optimization, and mental clarity practice all rolled into one.

BREAKTHROUGH requires regular sessions to clear your own blocks and patterns. Whether working with other practitioners or using self-guided techniques, this is your personal development, therapy, and growth work combined.

BUILD requires regular assessment and iteration of your systems, both personal and professional. This is your business development and habit formation combined.

This isn't extra work. This IS your business development and personal development integrated into one practice.

CHAPTER 5

THE BREATHOLUTION™ METHOD TECHNIQUES THAT WILL CHANGE YOUR PRACTICE FOREVER

I want you to stop seeing breath work and hypnosis as two separate modalities and start thinking of them as one. That is actually what The Breatholution™ Method is.

Think about the breath. It's a metaphor, an induction, an anchor, a deepener, a convincer. Everything you can do with breath helps us access the body's wisdom rapidly while simultaneously engaging the mind's capacity for change. When you combine conscious breathing with hypnotic language, you're working with both the 80 percent pathway from body to brain and the 20 percent pathway from brain to body at the same time.

These are some techniques you can start using immediately. But understand this: these individual techniques are nothing like experiencing a full The Breatholution™ session. To truly understand what this work can do, you must experience a complete session for yourself, where breath and hypnosis are woven together seamlessly for an entire journey.

5-5 Breathing: Your Secret Weapon

Every practitioner should use this technique daily, and so should your clients. This is what's called Coherent Breathing, also known as 5-5 breathing because of its simple rhythm.

The protocol: Five seconds in through the nose. Five seconds out through the nose. That's it.

Multiple studies have shown that doing this simple breathing rhythm for just a few minutes can reduce cortisol levels by up to 25 percent. That's a staggering shift from one technique. Think about what this means for your clients who are dealing with chronic stress, anxiety, or overwhelm. You're giving them a tool that can shift their stress hormones in real time.

Now imagine if your clients did this for five minutes, three times per day. Imagine what happens to the state of their nervous system when they're actively reducing cortisol levels consistently throughout their day. Imagine what happens when YOU do it before every session, showing up in a regulated state that your clients can feel immediately.

If there's only one thing you take from this book, let it be this: self-regulate before you facilitate.

Your Anxiety Is Making Your Dog Anxious

A friend of mine, a chiropractor, shared a story with me that perfectly illustrates the power of nervous system co-regulation. One of her clients complained that her dog had anxiety, so she hired a dog trainer. They went for a walk together, and afterward, the trainer said something shocking:

> "Your dog isn't the problem. You are."

Confused, the client asked what she meant. The trainer explained:

> "Every time another dog came by, you changed your breathing, which activated your sympathetic nervous system. Your dog felt that shift and mirrored your panic."

This is co-regulation in action. Nervous system to nervous system. Now replace the dog with your client.

If you're dysregulated, your client feels it, even over Zoom calls. Your nervous system state is contagious. Embodiment isn't optional when you're facilitating transformation. You must be grounded before you guide.

Occupy Their Mind, Access Their Soul

Use this 5:5 coherent breathing to co-regulate with your clients. As the practitioner, you breathe in the pattern and ask your client to breathe in the same way. This is incredibly powerful during conversational hypnosis or live coaching sessions because it creates immediate rapport at the nervous system level.

If you're a hypnotherapist, you can take this further and use the five-in, five-out technique as an induction. When your client is focused on their breathing, their conscious mind is already occupied with this simple task. This makes it easier for them to enter a trance more quickly because their analytical mind has something to focus on.

This technique works especially well with people who are more analytical or left-brained. Instead of asking them to "just relax," which often creates more tension, you're giving them a specific task that naturally leads to relaxation. Their mind feels productive while their nervous system settles.

This simple technique has helped thousands of hypnotherapists around the globe have a greater impact in their sessions because they create the optimal state for change before attempting any suggestions or interventions.

Breath is a bridge that drops the client out of overthinking and into their body, paving the way for deeper, faster subconscious access.

We Can't Breathe in the Past

Another powerful technique we use in The Breatholution™ Method is breath awareness. Have your client simply focus on their breathing without changing it, just watching it, feeling it, being with it.

We can't breathe in the past. We can't breathe in the future. We can only breathe in the present moment. When your client is anchored in breath awareness, their mind is completely occupied with this present-moment focus, which naturally quiets mental chatter and creates receptivity.

Now, start doing hypnotherapy at the same time. The combination is incredibly powerful because their conscious mind is busy with the breath while you're working directly with their subconscious. This will amplify any hypnotherapy you do because resistance drops when the mind is focused on something as fundamental and natural as breathing.

Get Them Out of Their Head in Under 2 Minutes

Most clients come to us totally stuck in their heads. If you do deep questioning or NLP work, they continuously say, "I don't know. I don't know. I don't know." They're living in their thinking mind, disconnected from their body's wisdom.

This activation technique helps them shift their focus from their head to their body in under two minutes, providing immediate access to emotions, memories, and insights that were previously unavailable.

Always ask for consent before using this technique. Let them know this might feel intense. Tingling sensations, emotional release, lightheadedness, and energy movements are all normal responses. Reassure them that these sensations indicate the technique is working.

The flow in practice looks something like this:

Twenty-five breaths in through the nose, out through the mouth. Fast, circular, active breathing with no pause between inhale and exhale. Think of it like an internal jogging pace for the breath.

At the end of the 25 breaths: Full breath in through the nose. Hold at the top.

While they hold, guide them with language like:

"Just feel that energy. Feel that energy dropping back into your body now. Feel the tingling, movement, and stillness. You're coming back home to yourself."

Or you can turn this into a hypnotic induction: "Just feel that hypnosis now dropping into your body right now. Allow your unconscious mind to open and receive."

Then let them exhale naturally. Encourage a second round by having them take another full breath in through the nose and hold it. You can use this second hold as a deepener, giving additional suggestions while they're in this activated yet receptive state.

It's a powerful way to create both an induction and a convincer simultaneously, proving to both you and the client that something significant is happening in their system.

How to End So They Never Forget

As Wayne Dyer said, "There is no way to happiness, happiness is the way." This technique helps you conclude powerful sessions in a way that locks in the transformation and sends clients home feeling empowered.

Use this technique when you want to create an emotional connection after engaging in deep work. It works especially well after timeline therapy, regression work, or any session where significant insights or healing have occurred.

Twenty-five breaths in and out through the mouth. Let them know: "We're going to do some activation breathwork now, which might feel a little uncomfortable, like headiness or tingling, but it's all perfectly safe. Just trust yourself and the process."

Full breath in through the nose. Hold at the top.

Full breath out through the mouth. Hold at the bottom with empty lungs.

While they hold with empty lungs, guide them:

"I want you to use your powerful imagination. Place your hand on your heart. Use your hand as a magnet, and imagine that you're pulling your heart full with gratitude, full with love and grace."

Then add specific gratitudes relevant to their session: "Feel grateful for showing up as a better mom or dad, better partner, better leader, better colleague. Grateful for the courage to look at what needed to be seen. Grateful for your willingness to change and grow."

This creates what I call an emotional seal. Clients leave feeling elevated, grateful, and energized rather than depleted or emotionally raw. They associate the session with positive emotions, which makes them more likely to integrate the changes and book follow-up sessions.

For When the Tears Come

This technique is perfect after timeline work, deep emotional release, or any session where emotions have surfaced. It doesn't have to be grief. It works equally well with anger, sadness, guilt, fear, regret, or any emotion that needs to move through the system.

When your client is experiencing emotional release, guide them through this healing breathing pattern:

Two very slow inhales through the nose: first into the belly, then into the chest. They can place one hand on their belly, one hand on their chest to feel the two part breath.

One long sigh out through the mouth: "Ahhh." Encourage them to make sounds if it feels natural.

Repeat this pattern: In-in-ahhh. In-in-ahhh. The rhythm is slow and deliberate, allowing emotions to flow without forcing anything.

Now, guide the client with visualization:

"Use your powerful imagination. Breathe in a white, bright healing light. With every exhale, this light travels throughout your whole body, scanning every cell, every fiber of your DNA, clearing the last old remnants of that old emotion. Just let it go with each breath."

You can let them continue this pattern for five to ten minutes, depending on what feels right for the session. It's an incredibly powerful technique for integration and clearing. Many clients report feeling as though years of stored emotion were released through their system in just a few minutes.

To conclude this exercise, gradually slow your breathing and return to a natural rhythm. Give them a moment of silence to feel the shift in their system before discussing their experience.

35 Years Without Crying (Until Now)

Susanne, one of my certified practitioners, had a client who suffered from obsessive cleaning behaviors that were taking over her life. Nothing had worked. She had tried quantum hypnosis, NLP, traditional hypnotherapy, and cognitive behavioral therapy. Nothing made a dent in the compulsive patterns.

This client had survived horrific trauma in her childhood. Sexual abuse that had never been properly addressed. Emotional shutdown had become her survival mechanism. She hadn't cried for 35 years, not once. Her system had completely shut down as a way to cope with unbearable pain.

Then, Susanne guided her through a The Breatholution™ Method session that combined activation breathing with trauma-informed hypnotic work.

The floodgates opened. Years of grief, terror, and pain that had been locked in her system finally had permission to release. Tears poured like a dam had broken. The emotional release continued with the recorded session she took home. More tears. More releases. More healing.

After that single session, the obsessive cleaning behavior stopped completely. Just stopped. That woman finally reclaimed her life because someone knew how to work with her whole system, not just her thoughts or just her emotions.

He Shook Like an Animal (Then He Was Free)

Viki worked with a man who had been addicted to alcohol for over a decade. She'd used every tool in her toolkit with him: NLP techniques, conversational hypnosis, standard addiction protocols. She'd tried cognitive approaches, motivational interviewing, even aversion therapy.

Nothing created lasting change. He'd stop for a few weeks, then relapse harder than before.

Until she learned The Breatholution™ Method and tried a different approach.

During the session, his body began to shake uncontrollably. Rage that he had suppressed for decades erupted. Sadness he'd never allowed himself to feel poured out. Trauma he'd tried to numb with alcohol finally had a way to release itself from his system.

He cried. He screamed. He shook like an animal discharging survival energy. His system finally had permission to let go of what it had been holding for so long.

That one session changed everything. The compulsion to drink simply disappeared. Not because someone convinced him drinking was bad, but because the pain he was trying to numb had finally been released from his system.

One Session Equals Four Sessions

That's how clients consistently describe their experience with The Breatholution™ Method.

Why?

Because it cuts through the noise. It bypasses the mental resistance that keeps people stuck in patterns for years. It gets results where nothing else does because it works with the whole human system simultaneously.

When you combine nervous system activation with subconscious reprogramming, working with both the 80 percent pathway and the 20 percent pathway simultaneously, transformation occurs at a depth and speed that traditional approaches cannot match.

This Is Just the Appetizer

You've just learned powerful tools that will immediately improve your sessions and give you a taste of what's possible.

But I need to be completely honest with you: these individual techniques are just the tip of the iceberg.

In a complete The Breatholution™ Method session, we continuously employ diverse techniques like hypnotherapy and breathwork together, using them to enhance each other in sophisticated ways. We don't just use one technique and call it a day. We weave breath awareness, activation breathwork, down-regulation breathwork, hypnosis techniques, metaphors, and suggestions into one seamless experience that can change someone's life in 60 minutes.

These techniques will enhance your work dramatically. They'll give you tools that most practitioners don't have. But if you want to truly understand what The Breatholution™ Method can do, if you want to facilitate the kind of transformation that has people saying, "Nothing has ever worked like this before," you need to experience a complete session yourself.

Don't Try This Without Training

Before you rush off to try these techniques with clients, understand that to guide breathwork safely, you need proper training. You need to understand how breath affects the nervous system, trauma-informed facilitation principles, how to handle big emotional reactions, medical contraindications, and your scope of practice as a practitioner.

Even these simple techniques can produce powerful responses. Emotional releases, physical sensations, altered states of consciousness, and the surfacing of traumatic memories are all possible. You must be prepared to hold space safely and support integration properly.

This isn't about scaring you away from this work. It's about ensuring you're equipped to handle the power of what you're facilitating. The Breatholution™ Method creates profound change, and with that power comes responsibility.

Your Edge Over Everyone Else

You now have tools that can:

- Drop cortisol levels by 25 percent in 5 minutes with one breath pattern.
- Shift clients out of their overthinking heads and into their bodies.
- End sessions with embodied joy and grace.
- Use breath to amplify hypnosis and NLP techniques.
- Access stuck emotions that have been frozen for decades.

These aren't "nice to have" additional skills. This is your competitive edge. This is what separates practitioners who get breakthrough results from those who struggle with resistant clients and incomplete sessions.

You now have the tools. The question is: Will you use them?

Start today. Regulate your own nervous system before you facilitate others. Test these techniques on yourself first. Feel the difference in your own body, then share that gift with your clients.

And watch your sessions transform forever.

In the next chapter, we'll explore exactly how this individual transformation work scales into group experiences that can change hundreds of lives while building the business you actually want, rather than the exhausting practice that's burning you out.

CHAPTER 6

CONGRATS, YOU CREATED A JOB (NOT A BUSINESS)

It was 11 PM. I was at the kitchen table. Exhausted.

I'd just finished working construction all day to pay the bills, then seeing clients in the evening. My body ached. My mind was fried. And worst of all? I'd lost the joy of doing this transformational work I loved.

The math was brutal: Never a consistent flow of clients. Always on the hamster wheel of market, attract, serve, repeat. Never enough income to leave construction behind.

I realized I hadn't built a business. I'd created two jobs. And together, they were killing me.

I've read that only 5 percent of coaches around the world actually make money. 95 percent essentially work for free. Only 2 percent make enough to live from it.

98 percent of trained, brilliant, talented, caring people, are struggling financially.

Why?

Because helping people isn't a business model. It's a calling. And callings don't pay the bills unless you add strategy.

The Four Essentials To Succeed

Look, if you're a coach, practitioner, or healer who's comfortable making $50 per session as a side gig, all good. I respect you. But this is for you if you want real freedom. The kind where you wake up in Bali, open your laptop, and facilitate life changing sessions for clients who found you because of your reputation, not your zip code. Where you choose who you work with based on alignment, not desperation. Where you can pack up and work from Byron Bay next month, Europe next year, or simply your own backyard tomorrow.

To build this kind of six-figure business, I needed to master four essentials.

I want you to ask yourself this question: Do you feel you have all four of the following essentials?

Most practitioners might have one or two, but without all four, you won't be able to build this kind of business.

- **The Mindset:** Not positive thinking. I mean actual nervous system regulation. Your breathing patterns determine your nervous system state. Your nervous system creates your reality. A dysregulated nervous system creates a chaotic business. When you're operating from fight, flight, freeze, or fawn, you make terrible business decisions, attract the wrong clients, and sabotage opportunities right before they materialize.

- **The Modality or Product:** Something with a genuine wow factor. Something that creates an undeniable transformation that people can't stop talking about. For me, that was discovering The Breatholution™ Method. Yes, I know hypnosis and NLP are powerful, but this integration is next level. The combination makes people say, "Holy shit, what just happened? I've never experienced anything like this before."

- **The Strategy:** This is probably where most coaches fail. And the reason why I wrote this chapter. I want to show you the things that helped me get into the 2 percent and scaled to a multiple six-figure business. Strategy without the first three components is just busy work. But when you have all four working together, magic happens.

- **Growth Environment:** This could be the most important one, and it's what most practitioners completely ignore. You will never outrun your herd. If you're still the lone wolf trying to figure everything out by yourself, chances are slim.

You need to put yourself into rooms with bigger minds and people who are preferably a little bit further down the line than you so they can pull yourself up to them. That's what changed everything for me.

When I was working construction and struggling as a hypnotherapist, I was surrounded by people who thought my dreams were unrealistic. They meant well, but their ceiling became my ceiling. Their beliefs about what was possible became my beliefs about what was possible.

Everything shifted when I started investing in masterminds, attending events, and connecting with coaches who were already living the life I wanted. Not because they gave me some secret formula, but because being around them expanded my sense of what was possible. Their normal became my new normal.

If everyone in your circle thinks $100 per session is expensive, you'll struggle to charge $200. If your family or friends think online programs are scams, you'll never build one. If your community believes that healers should struggle financially, guess what your bank account will look like?

But when you surround yourself with practitioners charging

$5,000 for programs, running successful group classes, and traveling the world with their businesses, something magical happens. Your nervous system recalibrates to their level. What seemed impossible becomes inevitable.

The community you choose will either lift you up or drag you down. There's no neutral. Choose wisely.

The Breathwork Breakthrough

When I discovered how to combine breathwork with hypnosis, when The Breatholution™ Method was born, suddenly groups weren't just possible. They were freaking magical.

Why? Because you can't fake breathwork. When your whole body is tingling, shaking, vibrating with energy, when emotions are flowing, when people are crying or releasing decades of stored tension, when you're in the experience rather than thinking about it, skepticism disappears completely.

I've held space for the most analytical and critical people you can imagine. I remember one team-building event where I was invited to run breathwork and ice baths for tradies, construction workers who pride themselves on being tough and skeptical of anything that seems "woo-woo."

When I started the pre-talk, I saw them rolling their eyes and laughing with each other, clearly thinking this was going to be some hippie nonsense they'd have to endure.

Fifteen minutes later? They were crying. Grown men who hadn't shown emotion in decades were sobbing as years of suppressed feelings finally had permission to move through their systems.

That kind of transformation is what I'm talking about. That immediate, undeniable, life-changing experience that skeptics can't argue with because they're living it.

I remember my first workshop in the Netherlands, where three ladies came back the next day to the yoga studio and told the owner they wanted to be on the waiting list for the next time I would come back and do a session. They couldn't wait to experience it again.

That's the kind of impact I'm talking about. That's what happens when you give people something their body recognizes as profoundly healing.

All of a sudden, I had way more opportunities opening up. Think about local venues: yoga studios, fitness studios, wellness centers, and retreats. They all need unique workshops that deliver real results. Corporate offices crave stress management solutions that actually work. Hotels host wellness weekends and need facilitators who can create transformation, not just relaxation.

Online possibilities opened up, too: No geographic limits. Global reach. Time zone flexibility. Lower overhead costs. The internet made the whole world my potential practice area.

But that's not the whole solution. There's more that needs to be in place for this to work as a real business.

General Practitioner vs Specialist

"I help with anxiety, depression, trauma, relationships, addiction, confidence, money blocks, spiritual awakening, chronic pain, insomnia, weight loss, smoking cessation..."

That was my website. My elevator pitch. My problem.

Think about the difference between a general practitioner and a specialist. How much do you think the average wages of a GP compare to those of an eye specialist or a heart surgeon?

Exactly. Dramatically different positioning leads to dramatically different income.

When you specialize, you become the authority in that specific area. You master one transformation instead of dabbling in many different problems. Repetition is the mother of skill, so you get better and better at solving one specific problem. Your results improve because you're not spreading your attention across ten different issues. Your confidence soars because you know exactly what you're doing. Your reputation spreads because people know what to refer you for.

When you try to help everyone with everything, you connect with no one. Your marketing becomes confused. Your message becomes muddy and generic. Confused people don't buy. Period.

But when you get specific, when you own one particular transformation, everything becomes easier. Your content writes itself because you know exactly what your people struggle with. Your workshops fill naturally because you're speaking directly to a specific pain point. Your offers become obvious because you know exactly what result people want.

The Temporary Ideal Client Revolution

Look, people get so twisted up about the whole niche thing. And I get it. As hypnotherapists, we know hypnosis can help with everything. But that's also the problem. Here's what I tell my clients: stop overthinking it and start looking inward. Don't complicate this. We're just buying time here, figuring out where to start.

Think about it: what was your biggest struggle a year ago? Two years ago or maybe even Ten years ago? Something significant that you've since overcome or mastered. Something you're now passionate about because you know the journey so well.

If you conquered social anxiety and now you light up talking about confidence, maybe that's your clue. If you broke through your own limiting beliefs around money and now you can't stop sharing what you learned, maybe that's it. Your breakthrough isn't just your story. It's your road map for helping others walk the same path.

The thing you overcame? The transformation you're most proud of? The change that lit you up from the inside? That passion you feel when you talk about it that's not just enthusiasm. That's your compass pointing toward where to start.

When I coach people in the business part of my program, I stopped saying the word "niche" altogether because they feel so much pressure. It feels like they're marrying the niche when it's just dating. It's just figuring out where you both fit.

So I call it your Temporary Ideal Client. Emphasis on *temporary*.

The shift happened when I stopped trying to help everyone and started focusing on practitioners who were exactly where I'd been: talented but struggling, certified but not confident, transforming lives but not making a living.

Transforming lives but not making a living. Let that sink in.

Suddenly, everything clicked:

- Content wrote itself because I knew their exact struggles and pain points. I'd lived every frustration they were experiencing.

- Workshops filled naturally because I was speaking their language, addressing their specific challenges rather than generic problems.

- Offers became obvious because I knew exactly what they needed. I'd needed the same things when I was in their position.

- My confidence soared because I was the perfect person to help them. I'd walked the exact path they were trying to walk.

Action precedes clarity. You'll find your people by serving people, then noticing who lights you up, who gets the best results, and who you'd work with for free because the transformation is so rewarding.

If you don't jump out of bed with a burning desire to serve these people, it's not your niche. Period!

Create an Irresistible Offer

Another thing I had to learn: Everything should be reverse engineered from your offer. Your content, your workshops, your social media posts, your networking conversations. All roads should lead to one clear, compelling offer that people can't wait to say yes to.

Let me show you what I mean by reverse-engineering from your offer. Let's say you want to help burned-out corporate women release stress and reclaim their energy. Here's how you'd build everything from that offer:

- **Your offer might be:** "The Stress-Free Executive: A 30 day program that helps corporate women release chronic stress and triple their energy without medication or time-consuming routines."

- **Your content reverse-engineers from this:** posts about stress physiology, videos with tips and techniques for busy professionals, and posts about energy management for high achievers. Tell stories. Be relatable. That's what sparks conversation.

- **Your workshops reverse-engineer from this:** "Breathe Your Way to Better Performance: A 2-hour workshop for corporate women ready to manage stress naturally."

- **Your networking conversations reverse-engineer from this:** "I help corporate women who are burning out learn how to manage stress in 30 days so they can reclaim their energy and perform at their peak."

See the difference between this focused approach and saying, "I do hypnotherapy sessions"?

Don't say "I do hypnotherapy sessions" or "I'm a life coach." That tells people nothing about the specific result you create or who you serve.

Say something like: "I help burned-out corporate women release stress in 30 days without medication." Or "I help women over 40 reclaim their body, confidence, and radiance after years of self-neglect" Or "I help parents regulate their nervous systems so they can have better relationships with their children."

The difference is night and day. The first approach makes people think, "So what?" The second approach makes your ideal clients think, "That's exactly what I need."

Your workshops, your content, your conversations, all roads lead to your irresistible offer.

Why? Because the number one buying factor for clients is *certainty*. If you're not crystal clear on your offer, you can't present it with certainty. Without certainty, nobody buys. You don't feel confident in your pitch. And your motivation drops because you're not sure what you're actually selling.

High-Ticket vs. Low-Ticket

Before we dive into pricing strategy, I need to address something important. If you hear terms like "high ticket," "premium prices," or "charging what you're worth" and you feel triggered, angry, or resistant, that means your nervous system has trapped emotions around money. These are money blocks stuck in your system that need to be cleared.

I identified this in my own healing journey. I became angry when people started talking about money and the prices they would charge. That anger was my nervous system's way of protecting me from feeling the pain of my own financial struggles and limiting beliefs about what I deserved.

If this is happening for you, don't skip this section. Read it anyway. Your triggers are showing you exactly what needs to be healed.

Let me share something that might trigger you: *It takes the same energy to sell a $200 session as a $2,000 program.*

Actually, it takes LESS energy to sell high-ticket because the clients are completely different:

Low-ticket clients haggle over price before they even know what you do. The ones that cancel at the last minute because "something came up." They don't do the work you give them between sessions. They expect miracles without putting in effort. They drain your energy and leave you feeling exhausted and resentful.

High-ticket clients value the transformation and understand that quality costs money. They show up fully to every session and implement everything you suggest. They get incredible results because they're invested in the process. They become raving fans who refer you to their friends and family. They energize you because working with them feels like a collaboration rather than a battle.

When you charge what you're worth, you attract people who are worth your time.

But here's the secret to high-ticket: Your offer has to be absolutely irresistible. It has to solve an urgent problem that your ideal clients desperately want fixed. And it has to be positioned in a way that makes saying yes feel easier than saying no.

The Living Proof

This isn't a theory. This is what happens when practitioners get all four essentials working together: the regulated nervous system, the powerful modality, the strategic approach, and the community that pulls them up to the next level.

Let me share some real examples from my program:

Ege had no hypnotherapy background when she started, just some personal development work and a genuine desire to help people. She was working mainly for free and dreamed of doing transformation work full-time. *She made $9,000 in her first two months in our program.* Not be cause she was special or had some natural gift, but because she followed the system: regulated her nervous system daily, mastered The Breatholution™ Method, got crystal clear on her ideal client and offer, and surrounded herself with other practitioners who were already succeeding at this level.

Karen was a trained hypnotherapist who'd been struggling to fill her practice for over a year. She had the skills but not the business strategy or the community support. *She generated $10,000 in her first month after learning how to position herself as a specialist and created an irresistible offer.* She went from begging people to book sessions to having a waiting list. The transformation happened when she joined a community of practitioners who normalized charging premium prices and supported each other's growth.

Dave was a breathwork facilitator who was giving his sessions away for practically nothing because he didn't understand his value and was surrounded by people who thought healers should struggle financially. He made $5,000 from his very first workshop after learning how to price and position his work properly and connecting with practitioners who were already running successful workshops. One workshop generated more income than he'd made in the previous six months combined.

And Sonja? *She earned $16,000 from a single five-day online event.* She took everything she'd learned about group facilitation, online delivery, and premium positioning and created an experience that people traveled internationally to attend virtually. But the real game changer was being part of a community where this level of success was normal, not exceptional.

Where You Stand Right Now

Right now, you might be sitting at your kitchen table, exhausted and frustrated, knowing that something needs to change. Maybe you're dealing with inconsistent income that keeps you up at night. Maybe you can't figure out why your marketing isn't working despite following all the "expert" advice. Maybe you're burning out from trading time for money and can't see a way to scale.

Or maybe you're already flowing. You're already happy with your practice. But you feel that in this chapter, there are things that resonate, like the group sessions or the premium positioning ideas.

Either way, you have two choices:

- **Choice 1:** Keep doing what you're doing. Trade hours for dollars. Hoping that something magically shifts. Stay stuck in the same patterns that got you here.

- **Choice 2:** Get strategic. Master groups. Get specific about who you serve. Create an irresistible offer. Build an actual business that serves you while you serve others.

- **Here's what I know:** The difference between struggling and thriving isn't your talent. It's not your certification. It's not even how much you care about helping people.

The difference is whether you're willing to stop being just a practitioner and start being a business owner.

But before you decide, let me give you something concrete to work with.

Your Strategy Session Starts Now

Remember Ege, who made $9,000 in her first two months? Her first step was getting crystal clear on exactly who she served and what specific result she created. Let me show you how to do the same thing.

Before you turn the page, you need two things: your Temporary Ideal Client and your Irresistible Offer.

Take ten minutes right now. Don't just read this, do it. Grab a pen and paper or open a document on your computer. Your future business depends on the clarity you create in the next few minutes.

Exercise 1: Choose Your Temporary Ideal Client

Before you dive into this exercise, take a moment to think about your life story. What have you overcome? What transformation are you most proud of? Who do you feel called to serve based on your own journey?

Use the 3C Formula to evaluate potential niches:

- **Clarity:** Does this niche align with my personal mission, values, and expertise? Can I talk about this topic for hours without getting bored? Do I have personal experience or professional training that gives me credibility in this area?

- **Clients:** Is there urgent demand for this transformation? Are people actively looking for solutions to this problem? Are they frustrated with current options and willing to try something new?

- **Cash Flow:** Are people in this niche willing to invest in the solution? Do they have disposable income and view this problem as expensive enough to warrant professional help?

The test: Can you talk about this topic passionately for hours? Does it solve a real, specific problem that keeps people up at night? Is it specific enough to target a clear audience rather than "everyone"?

Write down your answer using this framework: "I help [specific type of person] achieve [specific result] in [specific timeframe] Optional: without [common method they want to avoid]."

For example: "I help burned-out corporate women release chronic stress in 30 days without medication or time consuming routines." Or "I help single mothers attract their soul mate without the use of dating apps."

Exercise 2: Rate Your Current Offer

On a scale of 1-10, how confident are you in your current offer? Write down your honest assessment and the reasons behind your rating.

What's the biggest hesitation your prospects have before buying? Is it price, time commitment, skepticism about results, or something else? Write this down because it reveals what your offer needs to address.

If you scored below an 8 on confidence, you have work to do. Your offer needs to be so compelling that you feel excited to share it, not nervous or apologetic.

The 5 Mistakes That Destroy Program Sales

Before you create your irresistible offer, avoid these common mistakes that kill sales before they start:

1. **Confusing message:** If people don't understand exactly how your program helps them within ten seconds, they won't buy. Your offer needs to be crystal clear about the problem it solves and the result it creates.

2. **Feels too risky:** Without safety and trust built into your offer, people won't invest. Include guarantees, testimonials, your credentials, and anything else that reduces their perceived risk.

3. **Generic and uninspiring:** If your offer sounds like everyone else's, it won't capture attention or excitement. What makes your approach unique? What can you promise that others can't?

4. **No urgency:** Without a compelling reason to act now, people tend to procrastinate indefinitely. Limited spots, early bird pricing, or time-sensitive bonuses create natural urgency.

5. **No emotional connection:** People buy based on emotions and justify with logic. Your offer needs to connect with

their deepest desires and frustrations, not just their logical needs.

Create Your World-Class Program Framework

Use this framework to design an offer people can't resist:

1. **Pathway:** What's your unique process? What makes your approach different without focusing solely on the modality? For example, instead of "hypnotherapy program," you might say "The Stress-Free Executive Method: a unique combination of nervous system regulation and subconscious reprogramming."

2. **Support:** What kind of support do you provide? Weekly group calls, private messaging, email support, online community? The more supported people feel, the more likely they are to invest and succeed.

3. **Accountability:** How do you ensure they get results? Weekly check-ins, progress tracking, homework assignments, accountability partners? People want to know you'll help them follow through.

4. **Payment:** Do you offer flexible payment terms, such as payment plans? Monthly payments make high-ticket programs more accessible to a wider audience and can actually increase your total revenue.

5. **Guarantee:** What's your risk reversal? Money-back guarantee, satisfaction promise, or commitment to work with them until they get results? This removes their fear of making the wrong decision.

When you nail these five elements, saying yes feels easier than saying no for your ideal clients.

Now, what's the exact outcome/transformation you deliver? Make it specific, measurable, and desirable. Instead of "feel better," promise to "reduce stress by 50 percent in 30 days." Instead of "more confidence," promise to "charge premium prices without apologizing."

Do this work. Get clear on who you serve and what you promise. Then watch what happens when you show up with certainty instead of confusion.

Your Next Chapter

I went from construction sites to stages around the world. From barely surviving financially to multiple six figures. From losing the joy in this work to waking up excited every single day.

Not because I got better at hypnosis or learned fancier techniques.

Because I finally understood that transformation without strategy is just a hobby. But transformation with strategy? That's a movement.

Will you stop trading time for money and start creating experiences that transform groups of people simultaneously?

How about getting specific about who you serve and becoming known for one powerful transformation, rather than trying to be everything to everyone?

Are you ready to create an offer so compelling that people find the money to work with you because they can't imagine not getting this result?

The world needs practitioners who understand this. Who can hold space for collective healing. Who can build sustainable businesses that allow them to do this work for decades, not just until they burn out.

That construction job I was destroying myself with? That exhaustion that made me question everything? It was the greatest gift because it forced me to find a better way.

Maybe your exhaustion is your gift, too.

It may be time to build something that actually sustains you while you sustain others.

CHAPTER 7

FULL CIRCLE

You've made it this far for a reason.

Maybe something in these pages stirred a truth you already knew but couldn't name. That the way most practitioners work isn't just outdated, it's incomplete. That transformation isn't just about changing thoughts. That healing requires the whole system: breath, body, mind, all of it working together.

And maybe you finally see why those moments of self doubt, when a client said, "I'm not sure it worked," weren't your failure. You were working with half the tools. Now you have them all.

Not Just Another Practitioner

You're not just someone with a certification hanging on the wall. You're someone who gives a damn. Someone who's walked through their own darkness to sit with others in theirs.

That matters more than you know.

The world doesn't need more certificates. More techniques. More modalities. It needs leaders who have done the real work and know how to guide others through it.

If this book did what I intended, you now understand what it means to work with the whole human system. Not talking about problems. Not trying to think your way to feeling better. But working with the body's wisdom. The breath's power. The nervous system's truth. The whole human system, integrated and alive.

When you truly understand the nervous system, everything shifts. You stop trying to convince people to change. You stop proving your worth through complexity. You stop wondering if you're "doing it right."

You know, because the results are undeniable.

People don't just feel better for a few days. They transform at the cellular level. They sob with relief. They shake with release. They remember your sessions years later. They send their loved ones to you.

Not because you followed someone else's script. But because you learned to touch what's real.

That's mastery. Not being busy, but being embodied. Not collecting tools, but integrating them. Not learning more, but landing deeper.

Every Session Changes a Bloodline

Here's what keeps me up at night in the best way possible, and what should inspire you about the work you're doing.

Every session you facilitate has the power to shift generations. Every regulated nervous system creates ripples that touch lives you'll never meet. Every pattern you help someone break stops that pattern from being passed on to their children.

Think about it.

When you help a father finally break through his emotional numbness, the same numbness his father had, and his father's father, you're not just changing one man. You're changing the emotional inheritance of every child he'll raise. Those children grow up with a present, emotionally available dad. They learn that it's safe to feel their feelings. They model healthy relationships for their own children. They raise conscious kids who know how to regulate their nervous systems from an early age.

The pattern breaks. The bloodline heals. Because of one session. Because of your work.

Or the mother who releases the anxiety she inherited from her mother, who got it from her mother, going back generations of women who learned that the world wasn't safe. When she heals that ancestral pattern, her daughter grows up with a different blueprint. A nervous system that knows how to find calm. A body that trusts life instead of constantly scanning for danger.

That daughter becomes a woman who no longer needs to be hypervigilant. Who can relax into receiving. Who can be present with her children instead of constantly worrying about what might go wrong. Who raises children from abundance instead of fear.

Or the executive who learns to regulate under pressure instead of exploding or shutting down. Their entire team feels the shift. Creativity flows where there used to be tension. Innovation happens where there used to be stress reactions. The company culture transforms because one person learned to breathe. Hundreds of employees go home less stressed. Their families feel it. Their community's benefit.

One regulated nervous system. Endless ripples.

When someone leaves your session truly transformed, they walk back into the world at a different frequency. They parent differently. They lead differently. They love differently. They breathe differently.

And everyone around them feels it.

You're not just helping individuals feel better. You're changing the emotional DNA of families, communities, and cultures.

Your impact doesn't end when the session ends. It ripples out in ways you'll never fully see. But trust me, it's happening. With every client. Every breath. Every breakthrough.

Your Next Step

So, what happens now?

Honestly? That's between you and your calling.

Some of you will take these techniques and enhance your existing practice. Beautiful. Your sessions just became more powerful.

Others will feel something deeper stirring. A knowing that it's time to master this fully. To not just use these tools but embody them. To build the kind of practice that transforms communities, not just individuals.

If that's you, you'll know. There's no pressure here. No false urgency. Just truth.

When you're truly ready, the next step will be obvious. You won't need convincing. You won't need to "think about it." You'll feel it in your bones.

That's how you know it's real.

Why I Wake Up Without an Alarm

Do you recall my story from the introduction? My five year old daughter, Irie, her voice breaking as I walked out that door? "Daddy, please, you promised!"

That broken promise became my purpose.

Now I take this work more seriously than anything else in my life. This isn't just my career. This is my mission. This is why I'm on this planet.

I no longer need an alarm clock. I don't "go to work." I wake up on fire to share The Breatholution™ Method with the world. Because every practitioner I train, every nervous system that learns to regulate, each and every breakthrough session that happens, all serve something bigger.

My goal is to see Irie grow up in a world where people are conscious. Where they walk around with regulated nervous systems instead of triggered ones. Where parents have done their work. Where leaders lead from wisdom, not wounds.

That's the world we are building. One breath at a time. One practitioner at a time. One transformation at a time.

But I can't do it alone.

You've Always Been a Healer

This work isn't just about becoming a better practitioner. It's about remembering who you really are.

Beneath all the certifications, the techniques, and the business strategies, you are a healer. You always have been. The person others came to with their problems. The one who could hold space when things got hard. The one who felt called to serve.

That calling brought you here.

Now you have tools that match your calling. Methods that create the transformation you've always known were possible. A way to build a life around your gifts without burning out.

The world needs you. Not another version of someone else. Not a perfect practitioner who never doubts. But you, with all your experience, your wounds-turned-wisdom, your unique frequency.

Your clients aren't just looking for techniques. They're looking for someone who's walked the path. Someone real. Someone who gets it.

That's you.

You're not changing lives because you learned the perfect script. You're changing lives because you learned to be present with what is. To breathe with another human being. To trust the process. To hold space for miracles.

That's not a job. That's not even a calling.

That's who you are.

Join The Breatholution™

If something inside you is saying "Yes, this is it. This is what I've been waiting for," then listen to that voice.

If you're ready to stop dabbling and start mastering. If you're done with surface level changes and ready for transformation that rewrites bloodlines. If you know in your bones that you're meant to be part of this revolution in hypnotherapy and breathwork...

Then let's talk.

I've created two ways for us to connect.

First, *scan the QR code on the back of this book*. It will take you directly to my website where you can book a conversation with me. Not a sales pitch. Not a webinar. A real conversation where we explore whether you're ready for this level of mastery. Whether this path calls to you the way it called to me. Whether we're a match to work together.

I only work with practitioners who are serious. Who understand that this isn't about collecting another certificate for the wall. Who are ready to embody this work so deeply that their very presence becomes medicine.

If that's you, let's find out together.

Second, I've recorded something special for you. A 25 minute One *Breath Per Minute Nervous System Reset Session*. It's yours, free.

But here's the key

This isn't the full method. It's just a glimpse. A single drop of what's possible inside the full Breatholution™ experience.

It's not just a meditation. It's a demonstration of how breath combined with hypnosis can work together to access states most people never reach. Of what's possible when you work with the nervous system directly. When you stop trying to think your way out of dysregulation and start breathing your way into coherence.

Download it. Use it. Feel the shift happen in real time at: https://www.onebreathreset.com/

Then imagine what becomes possible when you can facilitate that same shift for others.

The Final Breath

So here we are. Full circle.

Maybe you started this book hoping for new techniques. Better results. More clients. A sustainable business.

I hope you found all of that. But more importantly, I hope you found yourself.

The practitioner who trusts their gifts. Who knows their worth. Who understands that true transformation happens when we work with the whole system: breath, body, mind, and soul. Who builds from a regulated nervous system instead of a desperate one.

The world is waiting for what you have to offer. Your future clients don't have the time to wait till tomorrow. Not when you're "ready." Not when you've got it all figured out.

We need you Now!

Because somewhere, right now, someone is struggling with exactly what you can help them with. They've tried everything else. They're ready for real transformation.

They're waiting for you.

So, take a breath. A real one. Low, light, and slow through the nose, using your diaphragm. Feel your feet on the ground. Notice your heartbeat.

This is your life. Your calling. Your moment. What are you going to do with it?

The tools are in your hands. The path is before you. The world needs your medicine.

It's time. Make it count.

Make it beautiful.

Change the world, one breath at a time.

THE END

Printed in Dunstable, United Kingdom

67770023R00061